CW00872154

HELP!

MY FACEBOOK ADS SUCK

Simple steps to turn those ads around

By Michael Cooper

Michael Cooper and The Wooden Pen Press are not responsible for any monies spent on ads, expectations not met as to individual ad performance, or any other damages that may arise out of misinterpretation of advice, or poorly constructed, or damaging ads.

Copyright © 2017 Michael. Cooper
Published by The Wooden Pen Press

All rights reserved.

Cover Art by Michael Cooper
Editing by Jen McDonnell

TABLE OF CONTENTS

FOREWORD

Hi, I'm Michael, a full-time fiction author who has a passion for marketing and advertising.

I've written this book for authors who want to understand how to market their books on Facebook, or for authors who already use Facebook ads, but want some new ideas, or haven't been as successful as they'd like and want to up their game.

NOTE:

If you've come across this book, but you're not an author/marketer selling books, you may not find as much value in the pages beyond this one. Although many of the principles will apply, I can't personally vouch for their effectiveness in other markets.

WHY AM I DOING THIS?

Why have I taken it upon myself to write this book, when there is a bevy of information out there on how to create Facebook ads?

Believe me, I asked myself this question while taking a hard look in the mirror (and realized that I needed to shave). My wife asked me this question, too. I have a lot of fiction books to write and release, and my income depends on getting those done.

However, I kept running into folks who were struggling with ads, throwing up their hands in frustration, and walking away from this valuable way to promote their books.

Seeing so many authors out there struggling to get their books in front of readers—many of whom have tried Facebook ads and only saw money flush down the drain with no sales—made me realize that I had to do something to help.

As an independently published author—one who makes a living exclusively from writing—I am as much a marketer as a writer. That marketing work, specifically, cracking Facebook ads, is what has provided me the success I needed to become a full-time writer.

THE GENESIS OF THIS BOOK

I'm a frequent participant in the 20Booksto50k Facebook group, and there I wrote a four-post series about how to create good Facebook ads and tune them to make money.

Folks really seemed to like the posts, but they wanted more information, and Facebook groups really aren't ideal for disseminating detailed information with accompanying visuals. Not to mention how much time it takes to gather good visuals to go along with the information.

However, I did want to keep helping folks while not taking away from my fiction writing—or at least, making it worth my while financially.

As a result, you have this book you are reading today. It's much less expensive than a course, but it contains the knowledge I believe you'll need to get Facebook ads to work for you.

I certainly don't oppose great courses like Mark Dawson's, for example. They will teach you what's in this book and more, but it will cost you more cash.

I sincerely hope that what I've put together here helps you get the word out about your books, and grants you the same freedom it has granted me.

Thank you,
Michael Cooper

MAKING YOUR OWN SUCCESS

Why do I think I have the chops to teach you about this subject?

Before we begin, I want to talk a bit about what success looks like, and why I believe I'm successful enough at Facebook ads to write a book about them.

As I mentioned in the foreword, Facebook ads are the reason I'm a full-time writer today, and the reason my series of books has achieved bestseller rank on Amazon multiple times, and sold tens of thousands of books.

I am neither the most successful author out there, nor am I the best writer, but I have managed to earn an income that eclipses any prior money earned when I was a software architect and CIO/CTO.

If you've got the writing, and more importantly, the storytelling, part of the equation down, then the right marketing can give you a second stream of income, perhaps even major success, and the financial freedom that comes with it.

I manage many thousands of dollars in ad spend each month, for my books, and the books of other authors, and I do so with a positive ROI on every ad that stays alive for more than 3 days.

Most ads I run have a 300% ROI, and many have ROI up to, and over, 500%.

Success comes from knowing how to craft a good ad, but also from knowing how to spot a lemon and kill it, or figure out how to make lemonade. Success means that you aren't afraid to increase spending on ads, because you understand their performance, and the return you'll get on that investment.

I believe that my success with Facebook (plus AMS and Twitter ads) gives me the credibility I need to teach you how to profit with online advertising.

When I note that something worked very well for me, you can be assured that it netted me hundreds or thousands of dollars in sales.

I say all this not to brag, but so that you know what sort of success you can expect to have over time, as you build up your ad repertoire.

Some of my additional qualifications come from my long years in website building and product marketing. I have built, or managed projects that built, in excess of 1000 websites. Sites from small mom-and-pop stores clear up to sites for Fortune 500 and Global 2000 companies.

I learned a lot about the process behind building sites that sell, writing copy that sells, and moving customers through a sales cycle. That knowledge has proved instrumental in my understanding of Facebook ads, and what it takes to sell products on the internet.

TERMS OF THE TRADE

Yes, boring, but necessary. I want to get a few of these terms defined and out of the way, so that when we get into the meat, you'll know what they mean.

CONVERSION

This one is simple. It is the rate at which someone who lands on a page, or sees an ad, performs the desired action.

If it's an ad, then the conversion action is the click-through. If it's your book's page on Amazon, then it's the user clicking the glorious orange "Buy" button.

CPC (Cost per Click)

The CPC of an ad is how much (on average) you pay for a viewer to click the CTA on your ad.

CPM (Cost per Mil)

This is the cost per thousand (not million) impressions on your ad. I recommend that you pay per click, not by CPM, making this is a metric you can view on your ad, but not one that has much meaning here.

CTA (Call to Action)

A call to action is the thing that says "Hey, Click Here" or "Yo! Do This Thing!" on your ad or page. It's the "Learn more" or "Like" button on an ad, or the "Buy" button on a page.

Any good promotion (even a flyer you get handed to you) will have a call to action; something that the person handing it to you hopes that you will do.

When the CTA is clicked or followed or taken, that is success.

FUNNEL

Any time there are sales, there is a sales funnel. This is the number of steps it takes to get a customer (in our case, a reader) from first awareness of us as authors, down to the final sale.

Ideally, your funnel should have as few steps as you can get away with. More complex products require longer funnels, but that shouldn't apply to books.

KU "FULL READ"

When I use this term, I am applying it to the full read conversion of a book in KU. That is to say, if the book has 100 KENP, and you get 100 KENP pages read, we assume that is a full read.

Could it be two people reading 50 pages? Certainly; but when we're looking at read-through across multiple books, it's safe to assume that someone who read book 3 read all of books 2 and 1, so the math works out the same.

IMPRESSION

Impressions are, quite simply, human eyeballs looking at a page or ad.

PRODUCT PAGE

Though I speak mostly about Amazon, this applies to all the vendors. The product page is the sell page for your book; if there is a button that starts the process of taking someone's money in exchange for your book, that's the Product Page.

For most of us, this will be our book's listing page on Amazon.

READ-THROUGH

The percentage of people who read-through one book and go on to the next, or read-through your entire series.

CUMULATIVE READ-THROUGH

This refers specifically to the people who read-through from the first book to a given book in your series (or to the end, if it's used without specifying the book they read-through to).

BOOK-OVER-BOOK READ-THROUGH

The read-through from one specific book in your series to another.

ROI

This stands for Return on Investment. Ads are investments, and you want a good return on them. Your ROI is the dollar amount, or percentage, that you make back after spending money on ads.

TRAFFIC

On the internet, "Traffic" is typically synonymous with people's eyeballs looking at a page. In the context of Facebook ads, it means the act of using an ad to drive traffic to a page somewhere on the web (typically your Amazon product page).

WIDE

A book being "wide" means that it is being sold more places than just Amazon. As in a wide number of distribution channels

PART 1: KNOW YOUR READ-THROUGH

I'll warn you right away: part one of this book has nothing to do with ads. But if you don't read it, and complete the spreadsheet linked at the end, you shouldn't be running any ads because you'll have no way to tell if they're profitable. Unless you already calculate your read-through, and have your own spreadsheet, of course.

You should never make an investment without being able to calculate the ROI (return on investment). If you don't know what your return will be, you don't know if you're sending good money after bad, and flushing it all down the toilet.

In Part 1, we're going to discuss a series of 5 books, and how you calculate the read-through (RT) of that series, and why this is *very important* when it comes to ads.

I'm not proclaiming that you can't run ads for books which are not in a series (either standalone, or loosely connected books), but they are much more difficult to calculate read-through for, and, therefore are riskier.

This is mostly because our distributors (read: Amazon) do not give us the tools to know in what order our readers read our books. Without a series, it's very hard to tell how much total profit you will make from the sale of a given book.

Quite simply put, series are great because you only have to advertise the first book; then you can run it as a loss leader to build your funnel.

There are scenarios where you will advertise books other than the first in a series, and we'll get to that later on.

Now, as defined in the Terms of the Trade section, your read-through is, quite simply, how many of your readers read-through each book and then pick up the next book.

There are two types of read-through: Book Over Book, and Cumulative.

CUMULATIVE READ-THROUGH (CRT)

What does cumulative read-through have to do with ads and ROI, anyway?

The thing we are trying to determine with cumulative read-through (CRT) is the value of a sale of book 1 in your series. In simple terms, you want to be able to say, "If I sell book 1 in my series, I will see x dollars in net profit."

To do this, we need to know how many readers actually make it to the end of our hypothetical 5-book series, what books they drop off on, and how much net profit there is in every book (both on sales and KU reads).

This calculation is super simple for sales. At the end of the month, take all the sales of the last book in the series, and divide it by the sales of the first book in the series.

For example, if book 1 sold 876 copies, and book 5 sold 514 copies:

$$514 \div 876 = 0.5867$$

59%

This would mean that your entire series has a 59% RT. This is not amazing, but it's not awful either. Based on the authors I've spoken to, this is right down the middle.

To work out the net profits across the entire series, you need to do this for each book in the series (book x divided by book 1).

Don't Panic. The end of Part 1 has a link to a spreadsheet that will do all this math for you. All you have to do is plug in your monthly numbers.

If you're in Kindle Unlimited (aka KDP Select), then this is a bit trickier.

NOTE: If you have an omnibus edition that encompasses books 1-3 (for example), or just released the last book in the series, you will see the later numbers sometimes come out to be over 100%. If this is the case, you may be better off using your all-time sales numbers rather than monthly sales.

SIMPLE READ-THROUGH EXAMPLE

	Sales	Sales CRT	Reads	Reads CRT
Book 1	100		43000	
Book 2	65	65%	41000	95%
Book 3	50	50%	40500	94%
Book 4	48	48%	39800	93%
Book 5	45	45%	39000	90%

Cumulative Sales RT on the series: 45%
Cumulative Reads RT on the series: 90%

You'll notice that the KU RT is much higher than the sales RT. This mirrors real world experience (both mine, and many other authors I've spoken to). RT on KU is almost always in the 80% – 90% (or higher) range.

In this hypothetical series, the first book is $0.99, and the subsequent 4 are $3.99. They have the following KENPC values: 451, 511, 614, 499, 457. (KENPC is Kindle Edition Normalized Page Count).

If we work out the diminishing cumulative read-through for both sales and reads, and assume a KENP rate of $0.0045, then for every sale of book 1, we make $5.94, and for every borrow of book 1, we make $10.27.

If your book has been picked up by KU readers, and has gained traction there, it is very common to see one borrow for every sale. This means that a sale of your first book nets you $16.21.

These numbers are calculated with the correct royalties and delivery fees, so that is an actual value.

Fun Exercise

Sometimes it's difficult to view your page reads as books read. If you get your KENPC for each book in your series, you can convert pages read to books read, and compare your read volume between KU and sales more accurately.

The spreadsheet linked at the end of Part 1 has a spot for your KENPC, and it will show you full books read if you fill it in.

This is contained at the bottom of the "KDP Info" page for each book in your series.

Earn royalties from the KDP Select Global Fund

Earn your share of the KDP Select Global Fund when customers re
You'll be paid for each page individual customers read of your book.
across genres and devices, we've developed the Kindle Edition Nor

"Your book title will be here"

Kindle Edition Normalized Page Count (KENPC) v2.0: 480

The math here is pretty simple. All you need to do is divide your monthly pages read for a book by that book's KENPC, and you'll have the full reads value.

43000 (pages read) ÷ 451 (KEPNC value)

= 95.34 full reads

Seeing your KU page reads as full books read and comparing them to sales can help you understand the value, or lack thereof, for your books in the program.

WARNING SIGNS

If your Sales RT for book 1 to book 2 is below 50%, something is wrong. If your KU book 1 to book 2 TR is below 75%, something is wrong.

By "wrong," I mean something has caused your readers to decide they don't want to carry on. Usually, this means something pissed them off, there's a problem with your writing, or you have a cliffhanger where the **main conflict** in the story is not resolved.

I should note that you should expect to see very different RT values depending on price. If book 1 is 99c, or free, you will see much lower RT to book 2. If it is full price, as compared to the rest of your books, then you should expect an 80%+ RT from book 1 to book 2.

BOOK-OVER-BOOK (BOB) READ-THROUGH (RT)

This type of read-through is less important for ad ROI calculation, but I want to talk about it for a moment, nonetheless.

This is the RT between one book and the next. For example, if you have 45 sales in a given month on book 3 in your series, and 38 sales of book 4, you divide the later book's sales by the earlier book's sales to get your read-through percentage.

$$38 \div 45 = 0.84$$

84%

Therefore, the Book-over-book read-through (BOB RT) between books 3 and 4 is 84%.

That would be a decent RT, but perhaps a bit on the low side this late in the series. Most of the time, folks see RT in the 90% – 95% range later in their series.

Here's an example of a healthy BOB RT:

Book 1 –> Book 2: 50% to 75%
Book 2 –> Book 3: 80% to 95%
Book 3 –> Book 4: 85% to 98%
Book 4 –> Book 5: 90% to 100%

If you see a particular book suddenly fall off a cliff in regards to BOB RT, then you know that you've made a mistake. You probably killed off a beloved character and lost a part of your readership.

Chances are, your book's reviews will tell you what you did wrong.

YOUR KENP READS AS FULL BOOK READS

This is a fun little exercise to turn those arbitrary KENP read numbers into something more meaningful. It's also necessary for the next step; but fear not, this is all done by the simple spreadsheet I've provided.

Once you have the KENPC number for each book, divide your number of page reads for the month by the KENPC value for that book, and you'll have the number of "full reads" of that book.

Given a KENPC value of 514 for book 1, and a total pages-read of 45833, we would end up with:

45833 ÷ 514

= 89

This means that 89.16 complete read-throughs of book 1 were made.

Wait! You have no way of knowing that those page reads accounted for 89 full reads. It could have been 178 half-reads!

If you had the reaction above, you're completely right in your thinking. We don't know this to be true—especially on book 1. However, we don't calculate CRT for book 1, so it doesn't really matter that much.

We do know, however, that anyone who reads book 2 likely read all of book 1 – so when we calculate our CRT for book 2 and up, we'll still get a meaningful number.

Also, for KU, we don't get paid by the full read, but rather by each page read. Thus, for our net profit calculations, whether or not someone read the full book doesn't matter; all that matters is the page-reads volume.

Converting KENP reads to full book numbers is handy because it can tell you the value of KU to you, vis-à-vis how many books there your readers are consuming.

Again, fear not, all of this is in the spreadsheet linked at the end of this section.

TRACKING SALES MADE FROM ADS

You can safely assume that all your sales come from your ads, in one form or another. To know if your ads are working, you need to track sales from those ads. If you're selling no books, this is pretty easy to determine.

However, if you *are* selling books, and if you're trying out a few different ads, you need to know which ones are working.

So how do you tell how many sales come from an ad?

Officially, there is no way to do this. Unofficially, it is possible to get a rough idea via Amazon Affiliate tracking codes. Is this against the terms of service for the Amazon Affiliate program? Yes it is. You are not allowed to use affiliate codes on any service where you bid for keywords (aka Facebook Ads, Twitter Ads, Google Ads, etc...), so do it only at your own risk, and do it only to prove out an ad, and then stop.

If Amazon catches you at this, they will shut down your affiliate account; but the links you made with it will still work, so it is not the end of the world.

Ideally, you should have different codes for each ad so you can separate your revenue. You can do this by clicking on your email at the top of the page in the affiliate website, and then clicking on "Manage Your Tracking IDs".

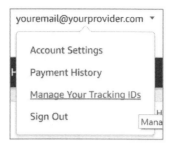

Then, on the following page, you can add new tracking ID's by clicking the "Add Tracking ID" button.

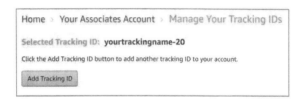

Now, whenever you make an ad, you can use the affiliate bar on Amazon to get the appropriate link for your book and ad.

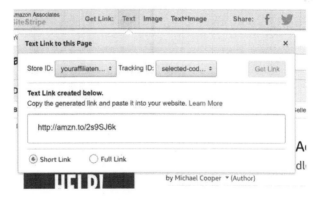

It's important to note that like AMS ads, there is absolutely no reporting on KU borrows and reads. You will have to assume that the percentage of KU reads you get on average applies to your advertising ROI, as well (more on that later).

*Aside for any Amazon employee who happens to read this:

We are not using affiliate codes to game the system or make extra money on the side. We are using them because it is the *only way* we can track the conversions on our ads. We would *gladly* use a system that didn't pay us affiliate money, but gave us real, useful data on the conversion and effectiveness of our product pages rather than affiliate codes.

We are begging you for such a service.

TRACKING KINDLE UNLIMITED BORROWS

If you're in KU, you can assume that some number of the people who land on your product page (through your ads, but also through any other means) are KU readers, and invisibly borrow your book.

But how do you track these fine folks? If some of your ad respondents are reading in KU, then they are a part of your ROI.

Well, then. What you need to do is work out the ratio of sales to your full KU book reads.

IMPORTANT: Do not work out this ratio by purely comparing sales earnings to KU earnings.

The reason you should not look at your ratio of KU reads to sales from a dollars perspective, is because books like your 99c first in a series will make significantly more in KU. Conversely, your later books at $4.99 will make more from sales (depending on your book's length).

This means that looking at the relationship of KU reads to dollars is not a comparison of actual books read—which is what we need to estimate a ratio of humans reading books, as opposed to pages being read.

Since you did the math in the previous section (or filled out the handy, dandy spreadsheet), you can compare your full reads of each book to your sales of each book, and work out the ratio of sales to KU reads, as well as determine how many readers are passing through your series in aggregate.

This is important because you advertise to people, not net profit numbers.

If you have 84 sales, and 89 full reads, you add the two numbers together to get the percentage of all your full reads that are from KU by dividing the total by the KU number.

84 + 89 = 173
89 ÷ 173 x 100

= 51.4%

But what we really need is the ratio. To get this, you divide your full KU reads by your sales.

$$89 \div 84$$

$$= 1.06$$

This means that for every sale you make, you get 1.06 full KU reads of that book, as well.

Because we have little data on KU borrows—where they come from, or how many we have—we can simply assume that a certain percentage of the people who you advertise to, who search for your books or keywords, etc… are just magically "KU readers". We also have to assume that the same ratio of "buyers" to KU readers is the same; regardless of the route they took to get to your product page.

In the example above, we assume that for every person who lands on your book's product page and hits "Buy," 1.06 people land there and click "Read for Free".

Because this is an average, we can (mostly) safely apply it to our ads, as well. For every sale you see logged in Amazon's affiliate site for a given ad (in this case), we'd assume that another 1.06 people also borrowed.

NET PROFIT FROM READ-THROUGH

Let's continue with our example of a 5-book series. We're advertising book 1, and we know that for each sale of book 1, we make $5.94. Also, in theory, a KU reader borrowing book 1 will make us $10.27.

However, I really don't feel comfortable assuming that so many KU readers land on, and borrow, from on my product page. I'm going to pretend that 50% of all KU readers get to my book by magic (as in, Amazon specially promotes KU books to them through an avenue by which it does not promote non-KU books). Therefore, I'm going to cut that $10.27 number in half.

Wait...what? Why did you just cut your reads revenue in half?

The base assumption I made, is that all readers are equal. If my ratio of buying readers to borrowing readers is 1.06, then I'm assuming it's 1.06 everywhere.

That assumption means that if I am walking down the street and I throw a rock, I'll hit one buying reader, and 1.06 borrowing readers.

But what if Amazon specially promotes KU books to those borrowing readers though some other avenue, and a large percentage of my KU borrows and reads have nothing do with my effort?

I honestly don't know; but to stay safe, that is why I cut my net profit from magical KU readers in half.

OK, back to working out our net profit...

I still multiply the 50% cut of my estimated borrows revenue by the reads KU ratio we worked out in the prior chapter, which means I multiply it by 1.06.

$$10.27 \div 2 \times 1.06$$

$$= \$5.44$$

And now, for our grand total, a confirmed sale of book 1 in our 5 book series, via an ad, will net us:

$$5.94 + 5.44$$

$$= \$11.38$$

COST OF SALE

Cost of Sale is a common sales and marketing term, and it's pretty straightforward. What does a sale cost you? Hopefully it's less than your net profits on the ad, or you're losing money.

What you will probably find is that about 30 clicks on a Facebook ad result in one sale (give or take 15 clicks). This can vary wildly, and the only way to know for sure is to use affiliate tracking. Again, using affiliate links on Facebook ads is against Amazon's TOS for their affiliate program, so you should only use it for a short time to confirm the ad is converting; even then, know that Amazon may shut down your affiliate account for doing so.

However, this is the only business I've ever been in where you can spend tens of thousands of dollars in advertising for a distributor, but have no insight into the sales funnel. Which is utter garbage.

Anyway, let's assume you see a sale for every 30 clicks on a Facebook ad. This means that the highest cost per click you can tolerate is the result of some simple math. Take your net profit we worked out in the prior section and divide it by 30 (our starting estimate for how many clicks it takes to make a sale).

$$11.38 \div 30$$

$$= \$0.38$$

There you have it. Given our calculated net profit from a sale, and a starting estimation of a sale every 30 clicks, the maximum cost per click we can tolerate is $0.38.

If our average CPC is over that, we're losing money on the ad.

CLICKS AREN'T SALES!

I want to take just a moment to talk about this. I think a lot of people believe that if someone clicks on a link in your ad, or in your newsletter, said click will turn into a sale.

It probably won't.

The conversion rate on your Amazon book page is probably only 2-5%, tops (on average, when you're not running a promo or a new release). When I talk about a sale for every 30 clicks, that is a nice, middle of the road, 3% conversion rate.

Even if you have a great, amazing, rockin' 10% conversion rate, that's only a sale once every 10 clicks.

That conversion rate will also be affected by the price of your book. Free or $0.99 books convert very well. Higher priced books convert at lower percentages.

On the flipside, a lot of people who pick up free books don't read them, and even a lot of $0.99 books don't get read. You will see this reflected in your read-through.

Also, if (in our hypothetical 5-book series) the first book was at $4.99, and our read-through was the same (it would probably be better; the higher-priced your first book is, the more read-through you get), then we make almost $3 more per sale of book 1 in the read-through calculator.

However, your ads will be less effective, and you'll sell fewer books. Like everything in life, it's a trade-off.

A LITTLE ASIDE ON PRICING

The debate on pricing will probably go on forever, and there are as many opinions as there are authors.

However, when it comes down to it, there are some key principles at play:

1. People buy things more readily if they are priced lower.
2. People value things more if they spent more money on them.
3. Books that are free, or $0.99, can attract readers who are not your core demographic (because they'll take a chance and buy on a whim, when they may not have at a $3.99 or $4.99 price).

4. Lower priced books often get more bad reviews because of #3, above. Folks that are on the fence about your plot, character, or premise, may buy anyway just to give it a shot. Then they find out it's not their cup of tea, and they give a bad review.
5. You catch more flies with honey. This is to say that, for every single one of us, there is a massive untapped market. I saw the other day that someone did the math on J. K. Rowling, and determined that she had probably only tapped 15% of her demographic. This means that there are untold *millions* of readers out there for your book who have not yet seen it. They're more likely to see it if it is priced lower, and ranked higher as a result of more sales and borrows.

What do *I* do, you ask?

I price my first at $0.99, because I want *readers* more than money. Readers are great, because if they like you, they give you money!

READ-THROUGH CALCULATOR SPREADSHEET

OK, that was probably more math than you wanted to do, and math may not be your thing.

To make this simpler and a bit more foolproof, I've created a spreadsheet where you can plug in all your sales numbers for a month, and it will give you your net profits per sale and per read.

You then can add your expected profits together, and divide by how many clicks it takes to make a sale to arrive at your Cost per Click tolerance level.

This spreadsheet will allow you to calculate read-through in a series. There is one tab for a 5 book series, and another tab for a 10 book series. If your series doesn't have those exact numbers, simply input 0 for sales and reads for any books you don't have.

Also, if you have a permafree first book, put in 0 for the royalty rate.

http://hyperurl.co/fb-ads-roi
(You will need to save or copy it to edit)

PART 2: ADVERTISING CAMPAIGNS

Gah! Doesn't that just sound awful? It's so formal and market-y. I should say that I happen to like marketing—especially when I believe in the product. So I'm not bashing marketers, honest.

Nevertheless, the term just feels so dry!

QUICK STEPS
(If you're in a huge rush and want to skip part 2)

Go to the Facebook Ad Manager and click "Create Ad". Pick "Traffic" from the list of campaign types, enter a name other than "Traffic" in the box that appears below (usually your book title), and click "Continue".

Move on to The Right Audience (Part 3).

OK, that little aside out of the way, let's get into what a marketing campaign in Facebook is, and what it means to you.

A campaign typically encompasses all your efforts to move a particular product down a particular funnel.

In our case, that's usually the first book in a series, and the funnel is three steps:

1. See ad and click
2. Land on Amazon page
3. Buy

Or, if you're advertising for leads (email addresses), which I *strenuously* advise you not to, then your funnel is five steps:

1. See ad and click
2. Land on offer (like an Instafreebie page for your book, or a signup form you manage) and submit.
3. Get marketing email and click
4. Land on Amazon page
5. Buy

Typically, the shorter the funnel, the better it converts.

However, some products (like cars, televisions, computers, expensive enterprise business products) have long funnels because the seller has a lot of explaining, and convincing, to do.

We all know that the full extent of your convincing needs to be cover, blurb, price, and look inside snippet. That can all happen on the Amazon product page, so get them there as quickly as possible.

Note: There is a chapter below that spells out exactly why I think that advertising for leads (emails) is bad juju.

And now, as quickly as I can manage, here's the breakdown of the Campaign types we care about, and what they mean.

CAMPAIGN TYPES

When you go into Facebook's Ad Manger interface and click that "Create Ad" button, you're faced with three types of campaigns to create.

(https://www.facebook.com/ads/manager/account/campaigns)

What's your marketing objective?		
Awareness	**Consideration**	**Conversion**
Brand awareness	Traffic	Conversions
Reach	Engagement	Product catalog sales
	App installs	Store visits
	Video views	
	Lead generation	

The left two are in the "Awareness" bucket. These types of ads are for getting likes on a page, or making people aware of your brand. They are aimed more at products sold in brick and mortar stores; things like laundry detergent work well here. Those folks just want to remind people that "Tide Rocks!" so the next time a person is out picking up some detergent, that's the brand they buy.

These awareness ads are not terribly effective for us, but they can be used to build up fan pages, which I'll get into later.

The three methods on the right are "Conversion". Now, conversion is really what we want. We want to drive ads to a sell page, and have that bad boy convert. Alas, most of us do not sell our books on our own sites, and these ad types are really geared toward a scenario where you control the shopping experience, and can directly tie an ad click to a confirmed sale and an email address.

Oh, that would be glory; but alas, it is not yet to be for us.

We live in the center column, under "Consideration". In here there is really just one thing that relates to our goals: Traffic.

What we want to do is drive traffic to our Amazon product page. That page (if you have a good blurb, cover, price, and look inside) should already be a fine-tuned selling machine. If it's not, your conversion rate of ad clicks to sales (once this is all done) will tell you.

The fewer steps there are between the user and that page, the better.

Now I hear you all the way over here. You've got this *sweet* landing page you've made on your website and it is a thing of beauty!

I don't doubt you, but no matter how good you are at making a landing page, Amazon's product page has decades of *science* behind it. It's built to sell. Not only that, but it's familiar to your visitors, and probably more trusted. They like that page. It's where they buy everything from car parts, to shoes, to groceries. Leverage that.

Also, you have three clicks before users start to get all "meh" about buying anything on the internet. Your ad and the Buy button on Amazon are two of those clicks. If they had to open up the book, or dig into reviews, you've used up another one or two. Do you really want to insert your page on your site in the middle of that?

However, don't take my word for it. When you get your ad built later, do an A/B test, with one ad going to your page first, and another going right to Amazon. Put different affiliate codes on each, and see which way works better.

I'll be right most of the time, but I may be wrong in your case, and I am fully prepared to celebrate your success with you.

Often, people decide to advertise on Facebook for leads. This is a bad idea. The next chapter explains why you really shouldn't do that.

ADVERTISING FOR LEADS

(AKA ADVERTISING FOR EMAIL ADDRESSES)
(aka don't do it)

Let's face it: our books don't really cost that much. We're not selling high-value items here.

This means that the value of an unknown email address is the $ amount we calculated that a sale of book one generates, divided by a rough estimate of how well your Amazon product page converts.

SOME MATH ON ADS FOR LEADS

First, you don't get a sale *and* a KU read from someone you're doing targeting marketing at ("targeted marketing" being you have their email, and you are sending them an email directly). You just get one. So take the $5.94 we got for the value of a sale, and the $5.44 for a KU read-through, and average them; that gives us $5.69.

What this means, is that if someone whose email address we have takes action on our Amazon product page, and buys or borrows, then we can expect to see $5.69 (again, this is taking drop-off in read-through into account).

There we have it: regarding our single 5-book series, the *maximum* value of a *buying* email address is $5.69.

Not everyone buys (as you probably know). Let's stick with a safe average: one in thirty email addresses buys your book. You may see better than one sale for thirty email addresses, or you may see much, much worse, depending on how you attained those email addresses.

So, $5.69 divided by our 3% (1 in 30) product page conversion rate is 17 cents.

There it is. The value of an email address for this series is $0.17. That's it.

I know what you're thinking; I can hear it from here. "But, Michael, I can get less than 17 cents per click on a Facebook ad for an email address because I tie it to a freebie, and people click like mad!"

You probably can, yes; I bet I could get the CPC on an offer like that as low as 5 cents per click if I worked at it.

But here's the rub: your lead generation page (where you send them to get the offer, and where they give you their email address) certainly won't have a 100% conversion rate.

Let's say it has a 25% conversion rate. That means that every four times you pay $0.17 for the Facebook ad click, one person fills out your form to give you their email and redeems your offer. Now that lead just cost you $0.68. And we know, based on our conversion rate of email addresses to people actually buying books, that $0.68 per lead isn't profitable.

Here's the math on that.

Remember we guesstimated our conversion rate on our sales to people when targeting them, with a newsletter or other mailing, at one sale per thirty email addresses (again, you can get a real number by using affiliate codes—and you can get authorization from Amazon affiliates to use codes in email).

This means that we have to pay $0.68 thirty times over just to make $5.69.

Cost of sale: $0.68 x 30 = $20.40
Value of sale: $5.69

Using ads for leads is not a great use of your money. You'll find that if you do cross-author promotions (like giveaways,

Instafreebie, or Book Funnel bundles), you will pay something like $0.01 to $0.03 cents an email.

In that scenario, your cost per sale is only $0.90. SCORE!

This was a very long way of saying that you shouldn't use Facebook ads for lead generation.

Now, I bet there are people out there who have had amazing success doing this, and have built up a list of readers who devour their books. That is GREAT, and I don't want to denigrate it, or throw that success into doubt.

What I *do* want to do is give you the tools to know if your investment (advertising for leads *is* an investment) will have a positive return.

Remember, this whole book came out of me being greatly dismayed as I watched authors throw good money after bad at ads and lead generation activities, without getting returns that were worthwhile.

I want you to *know* what sort of returns to expect on your investments, so that you know what "success" means for every activity you perform.

PART 3: THE RIGHT AUDIENCE

If you've been working at this marketing game for a while, or perhaps have been writing to market, then this is not a new topic for you.

Audience is something we as writers think about a lot. Who wants to read our books? Why? What else do they like to read?

What we'll cover here is how to create Facebook's version of an audience, using some of the same tips and tricks you already know, and maybe a few new ones.

Of all the steps in making a good ad, this is the one with the most data; yet it is still a black box. You can easily find groups of people interested in other authors that you *think* are similar to you, but you really have no idea if they'll respond to your ads.

Though we tend to think of them this way, at its heart, your audience is not defined by categories, metrics, or anything other than the type of escapism they prefer to engage in. If you can figure out what sort of books your audience likes to read, you're in business.

If you've written books that *you* like to read, then this is a breeze: it's probably the contents of your own bookshelf.

SETTING UP THE AUDIENCE IN FACEBOOK'S AD MANAGER

Before we set up the audience, we first have to create the campaign. As discussed in the previous section, a campaign is a bucket of "Ad Sets" which are trying to drive a particular type of activity. In our case, this is Traffic.

If you skipped the chapter above, and are about to click anything other than "Traffic" when creating your campaign, please go back and read it to be certain you understand the implications of your decision.

Before we get to setting up our Audience, we have to make our campaign. Here are the quick steps, once more:

1. Go to the Facebook Ad Manager
2. Click "Create Ad"
3. Pick "Traffic" from the list of campaign types
4. Enter a name other than "Traffic" in the box that appears below (usually your book title)
5. Click "Continue"

THE AD SET

The Ad Set is a smaller bucket within the Campaign. We're not yet at the ad level, but Ad Sets contain a number of elements shared by all ads beneath them.

We can't make use of all the options here (such as App), so here are the ones we care about. These are also the only ones we muck with. Default settings are fine for all the other sections.

1. Audience
2. Placements
3. Budget & Schedule

I'm going to work my way up from the bottom here, to get the dull stuff out of the way.

BUDGET & SCHEDULE

A good daily budget to start with is $5. The reason for this is that you don't know if your ad is any good yet, and neither does Facebook. Until you start to prove out that ad, you want to keep your spending low. I get into this a lot more in the Tuning Ads section.

Leave all the other settings on their defaults (noted here, in case FB changes the defaults)

- Run ad continuously
- Optimize for Link Clicks
- When you get charged: Link Click
- Delivery type: Standard (there are ways to play with this that we'll get into later)

PLACEMENTS

Here, click "Edit Placements" and leave "All Devices" selected, but open up the Platforms section and remove Instagram. It is possible to successfully advertise on Instagram, but it is VERY hard to measure, and we're all about measuring results here.

Once you have ads nailed down on Facebook, you can expand out to Instagram. Check out books like Jose G Lopez's "Instagram Marketing that Sells" to get a head start on that.

THE AUDIENCE ITSELF

Whew! It sure took a bit to get here, but I hope you learned something along the way. This is where we really get into building an actual ad; thus, where the fun starts!

OK, so now we're in the audience section, all you have to type is: "all the people who will love my book." Jackpot! Print money.

No?

Sadly, there is no magic bullet here, and this little box is the most powerful, and most nuanced part of Facebook advertising. In here, you can build an audience six ways from Sunday, and you can do it wrong more easily than you can do it right.

Let's start from the top with this idea of a custom audience (which, ultimately, I'm going to suggest you don't use).

CUSTOM AUDIENCES

Facebook knows A LOT about the people who use it. Seriously, stop telling it your favorite cereals all the time, kay? The data gods at Facebook have you all nicely categorized by your likes, dislikes, things that make you tick, and things that blow your stack.

To this end, they can take a group of people (be it people who like your page, or a list of email addresses you import), and find more people *just like them*! Well, then, this seems like the golden gun, the silver bullet, the cat's meow!

Inside the hallowed halls of the Custom Audience, you have two sub-groups. The first is a lookalike audience. These are built from people who have liked you, or a page you run. The other is a custom audience that can be built from Facebook pixel tracking or email lists.

People that you select from a custom audience can still be further reduced or honed by interests, as described in the next chapter

LOOKALIKE AUDIENCE

A lookalike audience is a percentage of a country's (or of multiple countries') population that "look like" people who follow your followers. I have not found these to be terribly effective, and I believe that it's largely because my fans may like a lot of the same things that aren't tied to books. When Facebook builds the audience that looks like them, there may be no readers in there.

This means that you have to constantly outbid all their other interests to get clicks on your ad, and you can end up having very high CPCs.

However, I also believe that you should experiment. If you have a fan page with over 1k followers and likes, then you can make a pretty good "lookalike" audience. Less than that, and Facebook advises that you may not be able to build a good audience.

To make one of these bad boys, you click the little "Create New" link, and then pick "Look Alike Audience". You can then pick from your pages and FB will go off and make that audience of people for you to market to. The defaults are best for your first run, but if you want to experiment with more than 1%, and other options, you should read their explanations.

CUSTOM AUDIENCE

Again, these are based on a fixed, known group of people that you provide. They could be from your Facebook pixel, or a mail list you import. You can even hook Facebook up to

MailChimp, and it will import a selected list and build a custom audience off that list.

These seem like powerful options that let you build out a group of people to market to.

Most of my successful ads don't use these.

The reason being is that I probably already know about these people. I have their email addresses, for Pete's sakes. Why am I paying Facebook to advertise to them, when I can hit them with my newsletter?

OK, that being said, there is one really good scenario for using one of these, and that is to advertise the next book in a series to people who have probably read the prior book. Maybe those folks didn't see your email, and you want to boost your read-through.

Normally, advertising book 4 to a general audience would not be as effective as advertising book 1; but in this case, you're advertising to your readers for them to read on, and it can help.

There's one other little tricky trick you can use with custom audiences that I'll talk about when I get to Social Proof.

The Final Word on Custom Audiences and Lookalike Audiences

Don't use them until you can build a good audience from targeting alone. They have specific purposes that are often not conducive to casting a wide net and gathering new readers.

LOCATIONS AND DEMOGRAPHICS

This section is pretty straightforward, but very important to get right. There are pitfalls in here that can eat up *all* your money, and give you nothing in return.

First up is the Country. Let's be frank; just pick the US and UK. No one else matters (sorry Canada and Australia). Focusing on Canada and Australia is like spending special effort to market to Florida...well, except that more people live in Florida. I'm Canadian, and I can accept this; I know you'll be able to, as well.

The exception here, of course, is if you have some sort of hyper-regional target for your book. In that case, you'll want to make sure you pick the right place—although you may find that Facebook Ads aren't profitable for that.

I used to also target Germany, but the KU page read rate there is only $0.0034 now, or something stupid low, so I don't bother (it's fine for German language books, because their words are so freaking long, but English books in Germany suffer because of that low page-reads rate).

WARNING: Whatever you do, *DO NOT* pick India or Philippines. Those folks will like and click your ad to kingdom come, suck up your whole daily budget, and you'll end up with nuffin'.

What I strongly recommend is making a separate ad for the US and the UK. For now, pick both those countries; and when you start getting clicks on your ad, you'll see why you may want to break them apart. We'll get into separating them in a later section.

Next up, pick your age group. I never bother with people under the age of 24—they're broke, and/or don't seem to read. Kidding; they don't seem to read *my* stuff. If you're targeting them, you should, of course, pick them.

Again, we'll get into reading the stats later, and you can see which age groups are most cost effective to market to. For my books, I start my target age range at 25-60 as a safe bet, and usually prune it even smaller once I get stats.

WARNING: Mindset Shift Ahead

Remember, your marketing targets may not completely align with your main reader demographic. You could have a huge readership (60% of your readers, for instance) below the age of 20, which probably means that they're not frequent Facebook users— you'll have to target them elsewhere.

However, 40% of your demographic is over 20, and are on Facebook. Well, well! Given population distribution, that's a bigger group of people; potentially millions of people.

So, remember, your ad is for a specific subset of your readers, defined by age, location, gender, and interests. The same ad and audience targets will not work for all of your readers. Probably not even for 50% of your readers.

Lastly, gender. You can't be all things to everyone. You probably know whom you appeal more to, so pick that gender. If you do want to see how you perform with both genders, go for it; but keep an eye on those cost per click stats (again, these will be covered in the tuning section), as you'll find that your ad may cost a lot more with one gender.

OK THE *REALLY* FUN PART: SELECTING INTERESTS

Now we're at the "Detailed Targeting". This is where the meat is (or soy... or cranberries; whatever your jam is).

If you've selected keywords before, this is basically your keywords section, with a twist.

The twist is that Facebook only lets you pick things that have significant fan pages/interest groups on Facebook. You can't select from 99% majority of indie authors, so here you have to pick traditional authors as your targets.

TARGETING BY AUTHOR

The simplest, and most generally applicable, way to target is by author name.

You should pick 2-6 of the biggest traditional author names that write books just like yours. And by just like yours, I mean their covers and blurbs look close to yours, in addition to the content of the book.

There's a ton of nuance here and its different per genre. I strongly recommend Chris Fox's "Write to Market" book. Even if you didn't write to market (or the idea is abhorrent to you), the same selection principles will apply for ad targeting.

When we get to ad tuning, we're going to get into how to tweak these interests and learn from your mistakes, as well as learn how to get the most for your ad dollar.

TARGETING BY GENRE INTERESTS

A genre interest is something that relates to your genre, but not specifically to books. A good example is if you were to type in "Romance". You're going to see a lot of options, and some may be a more general interest, but most are going to be actual fan pages/groups on Facebook.

A group that comes up when you type "Romance" could be about a specific movie, or a broader target, like romantic songs, that may contain a lot of non-readers (though this *can* be adjusted for, and I'll get to that). Luckily, for Romance there is a "novels" interest, so that should tell you that they're readers.

Another common genre target are TV shows and movies. Star Wars is a good example, here. I write Science Fiction, and so you'd think that Star Wars would be a great target for me, right?

Wrong. A grillion people are also advertising to Star Wars fans, and they're willing to pay more per ad click than I am. Also, there are probably a lot of non-readers in there.

However, Timothy Zahn is a traditionally published author who just (at the time of this writing) wrote a new Star Wars book about Admiral Thrawn. Now, he would make a good target. Excuse me for a moment. ;)

So, you can use movies, TV shows, and other genre interests (and I often do), but be judicious and do your best to keep them on target.

WORD OF WARNING

A quick piece of advice is that if your cost-per-click is SUPER high, then you are probably bidding for expensive keywords against a lot of other people. You may need to move down to a midlist author for your targeting, or remove any broad genre interests (like games, tv shows, or movies).

GET A GOOD AUDIENCE SIZE

As soon as you narrow down an age and gender, and pick a country (in my case: US, Men, 24-65+) you'll see a population count. That group is about 83 million people, from the looks of it. This makes sense; there is a pretty reasonable number of men in the US in that age group who are on Facebook. But all the 24+ year-old men in the US is a little general. Facebook's little meter is (understandably) pointed over at "Broad".

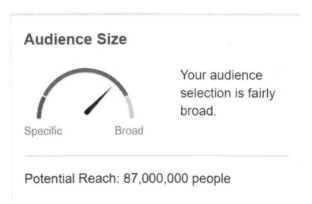

In the section above, I talk about picking your interests; but what I didn't get into is that spiffy little audience size count that shows as you hover over the interests.

This puppy is a big deal. If you type in a keyword like "SciFi," you'll see some interests with millions of people and others with 7. Be sure to pick the interests that actually have people interested in them (unlike the example below).

Sci-Fi   Suggestions | Browse

Science fiction movies   Interest

Syfy   Interest

Predator (alien)   Interest

AXN Sci Fi   Interest

Sci-fi Tv Shows   Fields of Study

LINK CLICKS
29 - 180 (of 610,000)

6,534 people

Demographics > Education >
Fields of Study > Sci-fi Tv Shows

Description: People who listed
their major or field of study as *Sci-fi
Tv Shows* in their Facebook profile.

I try to add interests and authors till I get close to a million in total.

Once you've gathered a decent group of interests for your audience, a little link will appear below this box with an option to "Narrow" the audience. Click that and add "Amazon Kindle".

What you've done here is said, "Facebook, target all those people that like *ANY* of those interests in the first section, *AND* like Amazon Kindle" (which hopefully means they read on one).

You can experiment here, and ad other variations of the Kindle interest, but *keep it just to Kindle!*

and MUST ALSO match at least ONE of the following ⊙   ✕

Amazon Kindle   Suggestions | Browse

Amazon Kindle   Interest

Amazon Kindle   Employer

Kindle Fire   Interest

Estimated Daily Results

14,637,600 people

Interests > Additional Interests >
Amazon Kindle

Even if you're wide, I recommend this. All the ads in this Ad Set target the same group, so you don't want to show ads to people who read on iBook or Google Play, and then send them to Amazon.

Once you get a good Amazon ad rolling, then duplicate the Ad Set and make an audience that targets your other platforms. This will also help you track your ad ROI per platform.

CONNECTIONS

Oh ho! What do we have here?

In this section you can target, or exclude, people who like me, my pages, etc....

When I first create a new ad, I often limit it to people who like my page. I want them to give me the "Social Proof" (aka likes, comments, shares) for the first few days, and then I go back and edit my audience and *exclude* them. No need to advertise to people who have already bought my book.

SAVE YOUR AUDIENCE.

Seriously. Save it. Whether it's good or bad, you want to remember these selections (especially if the audience doesn't work out—no need to target those folks again).

PART 4: CRAFTING THE AD

OK, I lied before; *this* is the fun part!

Once you've created, and saved, your Ad Set (which is where audience, placement, and daily budget all live), we get to the heart of things: the Ad itself.

There are a number of ad types you can make, but I'm going to start by telling you which ones *not* to do (I know, I'm such a Debbie Downer, aren't I?).

Don't do a video. Don't do a carousel. Don't do a slideshow.

The reason is not because they don't work; it's that they're either expensive, or time-consuming to create (or both). No one gets all their ads right on the first run, and every ad needs some tweaking. It's often cost prohibitive to tweak a video ad, and carousel and slideshow ads have a lot of variables.

I do toy with them from time to time, and I'm getting better at them; but even at their best, my single image ads still convert better.

ANATOMY OF THE AD

Single image ads have 4 parts:

1. The top blurb above the image
2. The image
3. The headline text
4. The description below the image.

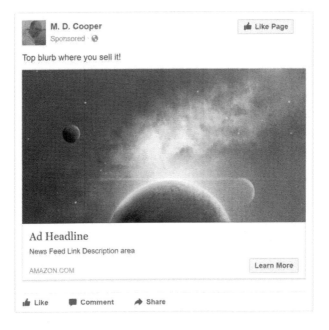

These four parts make for a lot less to play with when you're tuning the ad (than the other ad types, that is), and a lot less to have to put together when you're making it.

WHERE TO LINK YOUR AD

Before we get to how to craft that ad, let's talk about where to link it. Previously, in the section on not using ads for lead generation (email address capturing), I talk about the reasons you should always link your ads directly to Amazon.

In case you skipped that part, I really want to reiterate it here.

Remember the funnel. You want that funnel to be as short as possible (while still enticing the reader to buy). Essentially, this means the fewer steps, the better.

Getting that reader right to the Amazon product page, which is purpose-built to sell, is your number one goal. You should already have put significant effort behind a good cover, catchy blurb, and a good, grabbing peek inside; that being said, there are a few scenarios where you *might* want to send people to a page other than your Amazon product page.

1. You are advertising a multi-author promotion or giveaway. In this case, that page is your destination page. It's where the "sale" happens.
2. You are running some discount on multiple books. I did this recently where I discounted three books in a series. To facilitate that, I ran single ads that landed the reader on a page that listed all three books with links to get them on sale.

OK, so now that we have that out of the way….

THE TOP BLURB

The Facebook interface refers to this simply as the "Text". This is the section above the image, which I often refer to as "the blurb".

There are two ways to write this blurb. The first is to write it as "you" and the second is to write it as a marketer. The "you" version will be long, and should bring out your passion about the story. The marketer version should be about the deal, ratings, reviews, awards, etc.

MARKETER'S VERSION

This one comes in two flavors. The first one is what I call the "Pimpin'" ad. Here you're flashing pedigree, reviews, a great price; you're pimpin' that puppy out.

PIMPIN'

> *BOOKNAME by AUTHOR is rated as one of the best GENRE books out there. Top reviewer, NAME, said it lit his pants on fire! NYT Bestselling AUTHOR is bringing his/her/its A-Game, and you don't want to miss out!*

The Pimpin' version is best suited for sales and deals, because then people really just care about quick facts and savings. "Get BOOK by AUTHOR this week only, for just 99c! Critics love it and rave...."

You get the picture.

I find that this type of blurb does not work for a long-running ad, and puts off a lot of readers (though it works for some).

CHALLENGE

> *Is Michael Cooper the next J. K. Rowling? Pick up*
> *a copy and find out for yourself!*

Well that's pretty bold, isn't it? Some people may not be comfortable doing an ad like this, but they can really work. Just be prepared to police the comments as the jerks show up.

That being said, Facebook doesn't really care that much if comments are positive or negative. If people are engaging, they think it has value to their audience, and they show it more. Any comments are social proof.

Also, look at the stats for how many people chose not to have that, or any of your ads, shown to them again (which we'll get to in the tuning section), as you do want to make sure you're not putting people off too much.

YOUR VERSION

This one comes in a number of flavors. The first one is the "Flat Out You" version.

FLAT OUT YOU

> *Hey folks! I hope you don't mind me taking this little bit of your Facebook news feed, but I wanted to tell you about my latest book that is fan-freaking-tastic. It has dragons, an evil wizard, and a young lad who has to beat all the odds. I wrote it in an LSD-fueled haze, and it was amazeballs (the LSD and the book). You're gonna love it.*

This type of copy works best when you're making ads for people who have liked your page, or people who really have a close set of interests to your book.

These people already know you and your voice, and will respond well to it. Also, they are often just in need of a small reminder that your next book is out and waiting for them to devour.

These ads have the benefit of being genuine, which a lot of people really like and respond well to.

PLOT-BASED BLURB

> *Dragons rule the land and no one is safe. Even those who do attempt to venture out of their holds in defiance of the dragons find themselves attacked by the evil wizard. One young man possesses the power to defeat all the bad guys and save the day!*

This is the type of ad that people always tell you not to make. They tell you to make the marketer's ad; but for most authors, that's just not who we are. We're storytellers. That's our jam.

I say we should embrace that. Our readers come to us for stories. What better way than to get that story across to them in the ad? Tell them about the grand adventure that awaits them, of swordplay, or love, or desperate times!

You (should) have a strong emotional attachment to your book and why you love it. This is a strength. Use it.

When you're done writing this ad, read it aloud in a movie announcer voice. If it doesn't make you want to rush to the theater to see it on the big screen, keep working till it does.

CHARACTER-BASED BLURB

> *Jimmy has lived all his life in the Grimlock hold, scraping by to get food and shelter, and survive the daily rain of dragon poop. But one day, through some amazing circumstance, Jimmy discovers that he has a stupendous destiny that can save the world (plus the girl—if she doesn't save him first)!*

The character-based blurb is really just a twist on the plot-based one. There's a reason for this: some people prefer character-driven stories, and other people prefer plot-driven stories.

Chances are that your story is both. So make an ad for each element and run both. What you'll find is that about ¾ of the time, your plot-driven ads will resonate better with men, and character-based ads will resonate better with women.

That's not to say that women don't like plots and men don't like characters. It's just that gender is a fairly clear marker as to a *preference* for one over the other.

However, experimentation is key. Disparate demographics, markets, and genres will yield different results.

I had an ad that I was *certain* would not appeal to women, and so for five months, I only targeted it at men. Then, as I began to saturate that audience, I decided to duplicate the Ad Set (since that's where the audience is contained), added one reference to the main character in the story, and put that ad in front of women.

And it did great! It cost about $0.10 more per click than it did for men, but it was still within my tolerance for a positive ROI, and I reached a brand-new audience with the ad.

THE FUN AD

Who doesn't like to have a bit of fun?

> *Right after Jimmy finishes his after-school snack, he's gotta go save the world — or at least his town.*
>
> *That is if his mom doesn't make him clean his room first.*

He'd better get to it, or plant eating zombies are gonna be everywhere!

Ads like this really pair well with funny and food-related images. People also usually engage with them more; and the more engagement your ad gets, the less Facebook charges you for your clicks.

Obviously, you can't do this for a tragic book. But if your story has humorous elements, you can certainly pick out a few and make a fun ad that shows off your book's character.

THE IMAGE

Stop right there! I saw you grabbing your book's cover to make a little banner image. I know what you think you're doing, and you can stop it right now!

I'm going to start with the don'ts for you again.

1. No book covers
2. No slices of your book cover (like a horizontal slice that you cropped out)
3. No text of any sort

There may be an exception to this rule...

But it only applies to people who are willing to pay $1.50 per click, and I haven't experimented with it enough yet.

*When I do, I'll let my FB Ads Mailing List know
how it turned out.*

I can hear you again; you have a ream of reasons as to why your book cover will be the perfect thing for an ad. Let me explain to you why it's not: *Facebook* doesn't like it.

The good folks at Facebook have long-since determined that advertising images with words on them piss off their users (because, let's be honest, most people don't really *like* ads). Users who are pissed off from seeing crappy ads need to be shown fewer ads, or they leave the platform.

Facebook doesn't want people to leave just because they're inundated with market-y ads all the time, but they want to make money selling ad space. The result? They don't want your ad to look like an ad.

You're readying your response, aren't you? "But, Michael, FB now allows text on ads. I have several of them running right now!"

Yes, you may have, but my experience tells me that your ad with text on the image may be **shown less**, and **cost more** per click than the exact same ad with no text on the image.

I test this about once a month. I did it again just a few days before writing this segment, and it still holds true.

I took two ads in the same Ad Set, which were identical in every way, and ran them side-by-side. The one with the text showed about only one fifth as often, and cost over three times as much. This was even after I requested a manual review of the ad, so that it wouldn't have the display restrictions for being text heavy.

WELL, WHAT IMAGE SHOULD I USE?

Great question, glad you asked it. After I did my initial posts on Facebook advertising, this is one of the questions I got asked most frequently.

Previously, I mentioned that you shouldn't slice off a chunk of your book cover and use that. You're probably wondering why. You paid a lot of coin for that gal-darn cover, after all. The reason is that the framing of the image on the cover often won't work if you take only a slice.

In art, there are concepts like negative space, and the placement of main elements in the image and their relationship to one another. Also, som people feel uncomfortable if they see a picture of a person, and the top of their head is cut off. Color balance may also be wonky on a narrow slice of your cover image.

However, a good image that was specifically composed to have a balance of elements across a landscape (wide) image will be built differently, and will simply work much better.

The best thing to use is a straight-up stock image. You can get subscriptions on major stock images sites like depositphotos.com, and snatch up good pictures that fit your genre.

Important Consideration

These images don't really need to match your book. They need to match the genre, and they need to have good contrast to grab the eye on a Facebook feed.

I know this will really strike some of you as hard to believe, but trust me. I have spoken with many, many authors who spend as much as six figures on Facebook ads each year. This is how they do it: stock images, no text. Plain and simple.

A FINAL WORD TO THE WISE ON IMAGES

I ran an ad, at one point, for a science fiction series, featuring a girl standing on a ship, staring out over a starscape. You saw her from the back, with her head turned to the side ever so slightly. Great image, worked will with both men and women.

From the waist up, it looked very proper and not like something anyone would have an issue with. However, from the waist down, she only had thong coverage of her bum. It honestly bugged me, and I still might pay a digital artist to put pants on her because it's a striking image.

So, I uploaded the image, and used the cropping tool in the ad manager to only show her from the waist up. Submitted the ad, it was approved, and started getting clicks for a good price.

Then I started getting weird comments on the ad such as, "Well, nice picture, but I'll read it for the STORY." And others like that.

I didn't think much of it; people leave weird comments all the time.

Then, not too long ago, I used the image again. I flipped through the different preview modes, and made a rather interesting discovery.

Facebook crops the image differently for different placements (sidebar, Instagram, audience network, etc), and there she was, with her butt hanging out on half those placements…

Intellectually, I knew that the Instagram and mobile images are tall, and crop differently; but I hadn't ever uploaded an image before, where I specifically didn't want a part of it to show, so I didn't think to check.

So, if there is a part of an image you don't want to show (be it booty, or even just an element that doesn't fit with your story), crop it up the way you want on your computer *first,* before you upload it to Facebook's ad manager.

EXAMPLE IMAGES

Just some ideas to get your creative juices flowing. These images are all licensed from Depositphotos.com and Dreamstime.com. Only use royalty free images licensed from a reputable site.

HEADLINE

Chances are that if you put in the link to your book, FB has auto-filled the headline and the "News Feed Link Description" fields.

Don't use these defaults.

Make your headline snappy. Make it plot or character or deal based.

- Only 99 cents for a limited time!
- Save the dragon hold, save the world!
- Jimmy has just one chance at redemption!

This headline should be the punch that follows your blurb above the image. It's your big do-or-die sell line, but it also needs to stand on its own.

Now, over in the upper right, there's an ad preview section, and the default is "desktop" with little arrows on the right. Roll through those options to make sure your headline isn't cut off at a weird spot on some of those formats.

NEWS FEED LINK DESCRIPTION

This is smaller text that goes below the headline, which does not show up in all ad placements (you can cycle through the preview options I mentioned above to see it). A lot of the time what I use this for is to provide the yin to my blurb's yang.

If my blurb is all "raw me" marketing, then I put some character or plot stuff down there. "See what Tanis will be up against as she takes out the big bad and saves the day!"

If it's a character or plot blurb, I might put, "M. D. Cooper is an NYT bestselling author who loves kittens, and has been compared to Isaac Asimov and Larry Niven."

That's a bit short, but still preview it to make sure that on the formats that *do* show it, it's not cut off in a weird spot.

Again, don't be afraid to be funny in your ads if it fits with your books (which it should, if your characters are real, and are not in exceedingly sad situations all the time).

YOUR AD IS COMPLETE!

OK, it's not actually complete. First you need to pick your call to action button. I really wish there was one that said, "BUY!" but there isn't. I vacillate between "Download" and "Learn More".

The effectiveness of one button text over the other probably has more to do with the ad copy than anything else. Feel free to experiment.

But before you submit it, here's one last thing to consider:

SHAMELESS SELF PROMOTION

No, not for me; for you. That's what ads are. You are promoting yourself, and that can feel damn awkward. On the flipside, the folks who do a lot of marketing tend to *forget* that it is *supposed* to be damn awkward.

The more you advertise and promote, the more you start to think of yourself and your books as a brand. You detach yourself from it all and treat it like not-you. That is OK, and it's natural. I'm sure that there's some name for it.

But be careful. Your readers don't see you that way. They see self-promotion as a bit distasteful, and they like authors because they feel like they're making a connection with a human telling them a story. You need to keep this in mind as you make your ads.

Self-promotion works best if it's "raw you" talking right to the reader, or if it's a deal. They don't care if you're shamelessly pimping yourself if they get a bargain in the mix! ;)

PAY NO ATTENTION TO THE MAN BEHIND THE CURTAIN!

There is a way to have the best of both worlds, and it is to not run your ads as you. People will respond to a recommendation from a 3rd party far better than they do to one from you directly. This is obvious; this is why we do NL swaps, and use paid book services. It's why reviews matter, and why social proof is huge.

So how do you do it for your FB ads?

Here's the deal. You have your author page where you talk to your folks, push your deals and wares, and post snippets and cover reveals. This is you. Run your "raw you" ads from this page. Don't run your market-y/plot/character ads from this page, because they aren't coming from "you".

What you need to do (and this will take time, a good bit of time) is make a new genre fan page. If it's SF, you could make it about a trope, or maybe about some good books or TV series. If it's UF, you could make a Buffy fan page, or a general genre page like "Great Romance books I Love".

Run your ads as that page. Pimp other people's books there (good books that you believe in), and you'll build trust with folks who like and follow the page. That way, when you promote *your* book on this page, people will trust you and they'll check it out.

Pages

Keep in mind, though, you need to run that page as a faceless marketer. It only works if you create a marketing persona for yourself, and run the genre/fan page as them. Some people can't do that. If that's the case, work out a way where you can run it more as "you," but you'll lose some of the advantage of the "trusted recommender" promoting your books.

DO NOT pay for likes, or run giveaways to build followers on this page. You want this page to be true lovers of what you're putting up there. As you run ads as this page, you will get people liking the page. I know; crazy, right? People will click "like" on the sponsor of an ad!

It does take a year or so to build up a genre-based fan page organically (at least, it did for me). But when it's built, it will be just as powerful as a newsletter, and will give you an additional marketing and promotion avenue.

SUBMIT THAT AD!

OK, we're ready to submit the ad, so go forth and do it.

Some things to remember (and to double check, which you can do by clicking along the list of steps on the left side of the page):

1. Budget should be set to $5
2. Don't do Instagram unless you have already nailed Facebook
3. Pick a country
4. Pick a gender
5. Write copy like you're a human, not a marketing robot
6. **No book covers on your ad's image**
7. **No text on your ad's image**
8. Remember what YOU love about your work, and sell the emotion

Seriously, if you don't listen to any other advice I have, do #6 and #7. You will see better results. Guaranteed.

Your ad will take a bit to get approved (though it's faster when there's no text in the image), and then once it has, the stats can have a few hours' delay.

What we're doing at this point is seeing how the ad resonates with your market. If you have a killer ad, you'll know this in one day. You may also have a fantastic ad that will take 2 days to prove out. Expect to spend $10-$15 for each ad you test. If you're on day three, and the ad isn't picking up steam, then it's time to axe it.

So, how do you really know if your ad is working?

Read on, gentle reader, read on...

But first, here are some of my ads for you to check out:

A colony ships leaves Sol at the height of Terran civilization; taking with it the greatest, most valuable technology humanity has ever created. It is destined for 82 Eridani, where the colonists plan to build a new life for themselves.

The ship never arrives. Centuries slip by, then millennia. Five thousand years later, the ship returns—its abilities and power greater than when it left. It is the most coveted treasure in the galaxy, and the deadliest weapon ever imagined.

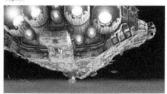

The Lost Colony Ship

In the spirit of great Space Opera by Peter F Hamilton, Jack Campbell, and Larry Niven comes Aeon 14. If you love strong heroines like Kris Longknife, then you're going to love Tanis Richards. Major Richards needs to get out of the Sol. .

AMAZON.COM

Learn More

2.2K Reactions 164 Comments 388 Shares

Major Tanis Richards will be up against the toughest challenges of her life. Not that she's worried, what with the Marines of Bravo Company at her back.

Outsystem: A Military Science Fiction Epic

In the 42nd century, the greatest colony ship ever built is leaving Earth...In the spirit of great Space Opera by Peter F Hamilton, Alastair Reynolds, Jack Campbell, and Larry Niven comes Aeon 14. If you love strong heroines like Kris Longknife and...

AMAZON.COM

Download

251 Reactions 20 Comments 33 Shares

Lara Crane stopped the rewind agency from controlling time, and hasn't used her own time travel abilities in years.

But that's about to change.

Someone she never expected has a little bit of revenge planned for her, revenge that is going to undo much everything she's ever worked for.

Seriously Twisty Time Travel Plot

If you can't handle twists and turns, stay away from Jill Cooper's 15 Minutes and The Bridge series. They'll melt your brain!

AMAZON.COM

Learn More

Tanis Richards may kick butt in outer space, but she's not going to do it on an empty stomach.

Savory Military Science Fiction at its Finest

Meet Tanis Richards. Terran Space Force officer, counterinsurgency specialist, lover of a finely crafted B.L.T. She's going to do what it takes to get the starship Intrepid outsystem—right after lunch.

AMAZON.COM

Download

29 Reactions 5 Comments

What would you do if you woke up 500 years in the future, lost, alone, confused?

You'll probably never know, but Kat does. She's just come out of cryostasis and her brother, her family, her entire life is gone. Even worse? She's some sort of genetic fugitive that the government would really like to get its hands on—and not in a good way.

Kat may have lost the future she once had, but with the help of Captain Wolfe and his crew of smugglers she's not going to take it lying down. Kat will find out what happened to her, and learn how to survive in this new future against all odds.

Science Fiction You Can Dig Into

Katerina Anderson and her twin brother Kris were promised a cure for their cancer, but there was a catch. The drug had to be administered while in cryostasis. Kat and Kris go under, daring to hope that they would have a bright future...

PART 5: TUNING THE AD

Before I get into tuning the ad, I want to talk about failure.

I used to work as a software architect, and the one thing we worked hard at was detecting failure—and doing it as quickly as possible. We weren't just looking for errors in programming, but also in our thinking. A slogan we adopted was "fail fast".

The same thing is true in ads. You aren't going to make a perfect ad the first time around. Or the second, or the third. Just like your writing, this is a craft that you have to hone and continuously improve.

Also, most of us writers are great at long form writing, and terrible at short form. It's just not something we do that often. That's why I'm a believer in the story ad; an ad that highlights your story and your storytelling abilities.

What "fail fast" means for us, is that you need to constantly look for ads that aren't working, as much as the ones that are. Also, *every ad will eventually stop working,* so failure is a state every ad will reach at some point.

SPENDING MONEY

The other thing we need to think about is how much capital you can invest in ads before you see a return.

Let's look at a moderately successful scenario:

You're running ads at $5/day, and your first three all flop. Each of those flops took three days to prove out as failures. That means you've spent $45 on failure. This is OK! Note what didn't work, and don't do that again. But ad #4 is ticking and getting you clicks at a good CPC, and sales are coming in.

Keep in mind, sales can lag by days, in some cases; so if you see clicks on day one and two, and sales in KDP reporting yet match up with in affiliate reporting, don't panic right away.

Because you're not made of money, you keep ad #4 at $5/day for two months. That's how long you'll have to wait, give or take a bit, until Amazon is going to pay you for those sales that you made when your ad started to roll.

At this point, you've fronted $300 on ads. Can you tolerate that sort of spending until you get a return? Be aware of that delay, and plan for it.

You can also pause an ad and start it back up again. You don't lose your social proof, though FB may charge you more per click for a bit.

OK, so failure costs you $45, and success costs you another $155. That's a good baseline to start with.

RELEVANCY – THE MOST IMPORTANT METRIC

Relevancy is how relevant Facebook believes the ad you've made is to the audience you've picked. What Facebook doesn't want is someone targeting 50-year old male bikers with tween dresses.

It's a waste of everyone's time and money, and it devalues Facebook's platform, so they want to put a stop to that by hitting biker-targeting tween dressmakers in the wallet.

Don't be a biker-targeting tween dressmaker.

Facebook's goal is to show ads that blend well with newsfeeds. Those ads should contain words and images that people *like* seeing because they're interesting, funny, informative, and spot on with a reader's likes and dislikes.

To this end, Facebook gives your ad a relevancy score once it's been shown 485 times. This score is on a scale of 1-10. The lower the score, the less Facebook will show your ad, and the more they'll charge to do it. I shoot for a 10 out of 10 score, but I'll live with anything down to an 8.

If my relevancy is under 8, I start tweaking and tuning that ad.

WHEN TO TUNE THE AD

The easy answer to this is: always. All ads will eventually lose effectiveness, and you want to have your next, well-performing ad ready to go. I even keep a few old ads warm so that I can turn them back on if my current batch starts to lose steam.

However, what you're really looking for are the signs that an ad isn't working. The first, as mentioned above, is relevancy. Shoot for 8 and above.

... ⓘ	Amount Spent ⓘ	Rel... ⓘ

Relevance Score

Overview   Details   Related

A rating from 1 to 10 that estimates how well your target audience is responding to your ad. This score is shown after your ad receives more than 500 impressions. It's only visible when looking at reporting for ads and does not appear for ad sets and campaigns.

| $0.09 nk C... | $72.68 | 10 |
| $0.24 ıst E | $20.00 | 8 |

Second is the CPC. This will start high and move down; if you have a good relevancy and result rate, then this will usually trend in a good direction. If it doesn't come under your tolerance level, then you need to tune the ad (Your tolerance level's something we determined using the ROI spreadsheet. You filled out the spreadsheet, right? Don't make me send you a facepalm gif. I'll hunt you down and do it).

The last sign is the result rate. This is effectively the percentage of clicks or interactions you get per impression. If it's below 2.5%, then the ad just isn't performing; you're showing it to a lot of people and they're just passing it by.

There are some smaller factors, like your frequency (which has to do with audience saturation), but that's something we can go over another time.

YOUR AD'S FIRST FEW DAYS OF LIFE

Before we get into how to tweak your ad, I want to take just a moment to talk about its early days and what you should expect.

I'm doing this because I don't want you to panic and mess up what could be a great ad.

A HIGH COST PER CLICK

The cost per click (CPC) on an ad is the *average* of what you paid to have someone click on the ad.

I could have an ad that displays a $0.30 CPC, but there could be dozens of clicks that cost me over $1 in there and others as low as 1 cent. Sometimes a bunch of those expensive clicks happen at the outset of your ad, and there aren't cheap clicks to balance them out.

You're going to see a high cost per click at the outset. Only ads that are *amazing* home runs start off with low CPCs.

Part of this is because you pay more for clicks before you have a relevancy score. Again, this is because Facebook wants to show relevant ads. In straight dollar click bidding, whoever is willing to pay more to show their ad wins and gets the impression (this is how AMS ads work, for example. Highest bid on the keyword gets displayed).

Here's an example. I have a huge budget for an ad, but a relevancy of 5. You have a small budget (which means Facebook has less $ to spend when bidding), but your relevancy is 10 for your ad. All other things being equal,

Facebook will show your ad over mine, and you won't have to outbid me to do it. That's because your relevancy is a part of the bid.

So, because your youthful little ad does not have a relevancy score yet, it's bidding for clicks at a disadvantage, and you pay more. This will trend down as your ad gets more social proof and, eventually, relevancy.

What you should expect to see is an ad that levels out in the $0.10 - $0.30 CPC range by its third day. It may fluctuate after that, but chances are that you can't afford a $0.39+ CPC.

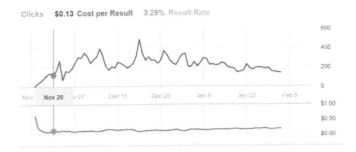

TWEAKING AD COPY VS TWEAKING AUDIENCE

These are the main two elements that are going to affect performance. Essentially, are you showing the right ad to the right people? Maybe it's the right people and the wrong ad; or the wrong ad to the right people; or maybe both are not lining up.

How do you fix one without breaking something that may be working just fine?

IT'S NOT ME, IT'S YOU

If your relevancy is high (8+), but you're paying a bundle for clicks, then there is typically an audience issue.

AUDIENCE IS TOO SMALL

Go back and look at your audience size; the number it shows may be smaller than Facebook said it was when you first built it. That happens sometimes. You may also see the little meter pointing over at the "Narrow" side.

Try to add some more interests, or maybe remove (or make a bigger) the "lookalike audience," if you used one of those.

I recently had an ad that I knew should work. Copy was catchy (made me want to buy the book) and the image had performed very well in the past, but I couldn't get the CPC below $1.50 (choke).

I looked back at the audience, and realized that I had used a lookalike audience that had somehow reduced my total pool down to a thousand people. In this scenario, Facebook couldn't find any low dollar targets, and had to bid my ad high to get it to show to these people. I took out the "lookalike" part and resubmitted it, and now it's settling down around $0.20 per click.

OVERSATURATED AUDIENCE

When you did your interest targeting, you may have picked the tippity-top authors in your genre/category; and so did everyone else when they made their ads.

Now, if your offer is good, like a freebie or some deep discount, you may be able to target those top authors, and have things work like a dream.

However, maybe you have another ad that you want to leave up so that it makes a few sales a day. That ad may do a lot better if you go down to some mid-listers in your category, or if you dig into some sub-categories and target authors who do well in certain niches.

When you do this, you may need to pick a few more authors to get a good audience size; but if it's a slow burn ad, you may be okay with audience sizes even down to 10,000.

Another option is to pick some authors of yesteryear. I often pick a lot of SF greats from the days of yore. They cost less to target, but still have nice big interest groups. Science Fiction examples of this are people like Anne McCaffrey, Robert Heinlein, and Arthur C. Clarke.

A great way to find these authors is to think of who was big when you were younger, or browse the stacks at the bookstore.

NOPE, TURNS OUT IT'S ME AFTER ALL

On the flipside, if your relevancy is low, then you've produced an ad that your chosen audience isn't interested in. If you're certain that your audience is spot on, then it's time to play with the ad and not the audience.

Another indicator of this scenario is good relevancy, but a low result rate (a rate below 2.5%). In this case, people don't mind your ad; they may be liking it, even commenting on it, but they're just not clicking.

So, let's get into tuning your ad copy and image.

TESTING OUT AD CHANGES

No one has a crystal ball (well, I do, but it's in need of repairs, on account of it not working), and no one knows for sure which ads will work best.

There are thousands of variables that can affect how well your ad is going to work. However, you don't have time (or patience, or money) to test thousands of variables. Even testing five or six different variables (multivariate testing) is exponential. Testing five variables means you have 25 possible combinations to test.

Nuts! Ain't nobody got time for that!

This is where multivariate testing's little brother comes into play: A/B Testing.

Here you take a SWAG (scientific wild-assed guess) at the biggest variable, and try two versions of the ad with that biggest variable being different.

I'll give you a hint: That biggest variable is invariably the image.

The image is going to make or break your ad before anyone reads a single word of it, so that's what we want to twiddle with.

STOP!

Before you go one step further, I need to tell you about what happens when you change an ad.

It loses all comments, shares, and likes.

That's right; if you change the image, or any of the text in an Ad, all your social proof goes poof!

You can, however, change the link, or the audience on the ad set—though changing the audience will nuke your relevancy score and you'll have to rebuild it.

OK, you may proceed.

DUPE THAT AD!

So, now that you have that ad made and approved, mouse over it, and click that little "Duplicate" link. This will allow you to make a copy of the ad.

In this new copy of your ad, you only change one thing (again, if your ad isn't working, try the image first), and then save it.

If you want, you can run both versions of the ad simultaneously; though you may need to up the budget in your ad set (remember, all ads in the same ad set work off the same budget), so that the other ad shows often enough to get relevancy in a reasonable amount of time.

You can also pause the first version of the ad and let the new version run on its own for a bit—though there could be time of day/week/month variables that come into play, so these results may be skewed if you're not running the ads at the same time.

Sometimes Facebook decides that one version of your ad just isn't something it wants to show, as compared to another version, so it just doesn't display it much. I've had this happen with images that did very well on other ads. What I do then is duplicate the entire ad set so that the version I want to test has its own dedicated budget.

You may also want to tweak the copy, because you're on a tight budget and trying out a dozen images is expensive. It doesn't hurt to do this (especially on an ad that just isn't working), and you could strike gold. Just remember to give your new copy a couple of days to see how it shakes out.

DUPING FOR FUN AND PROFIT

Not every image appeals to everyone. We're all different (thank goodness, eh?), and different things appeal to all of us. I often keep two or three copies of an ad running with different images, if they're all working. Something else I do is prove out several versions of an ad with different images, but then turn some off and rotate them, so that I'm not hitting people with the same stuff all the time.

DEMOGRAPHICS AND PERFORMANCE

As you've certainly picked up by now, I'm big on knowing whether or not something is working. I believe that knowing when something is *not* working is the most important of the two.

We only have so much time, money, and effort available to us in life, so we need to spend as little of all three on things that don't work.

Luckily, Facebook gives us oodles of information to help find out what's not working.

DEMOGRAPHICS

We can view demographics for an entire ad set, or just for an ad. Because we really care if a given ad is working, let's look at the demographics for a single ad.

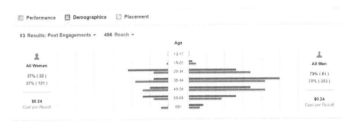

Click the "View graphs" link, and then click the "Demographics" link. What you'll see is a breakdown of men vs. women, and then impressions to clicks for each age group.

As you scroll down through the age groups, you can see what their individual costs are. You may find that certain gender/age group combinations are too expensive, and you can go back to your audience and exclude them.

You may also find that you have odd mixes, like an ad that works well with women 40+, but with men 20+. What I do in those cases is duplicate the ad set so I can target my best male/female age groups separately. I also often take that opportunity to tweak the image or text to be more appealing to each gender.

RESULT RATE

While you're in here, if you click the "Performance" tab, you'll see your result rate and cost per click per day. This is a useful graph for seeing where your ad is trending from a cost perspective. The thing you do want to keep an eye on is the Result Rate. Ideally, it should be above 2.5%; a decent ad will be in the 4% to 6% range. A great ad is 10% and up.

One thing that is annoying is that that the result rate isn't per day; it's over the entire date range you have selected in the upper right. Be sure that when you're evaluating an ad's performance, you are looking at just the prior seven days or so, and then comparing it to the ad's lifetime performance.

BREAK IT DOWN!

No, it's not dancing time; at least, not yet. We're going to head into some deeper data here about how your ad is performing.

When you're on the Ad, or Ad Set tab, there's this handy-dandy "Breakdown" button.

You can see there a lot of different ways to slice and dice the breakdown, all the way down to the state they live in, and the time at which they interact.

Some of this is duplicative of what you can find on the graphs and charts, so you can choose how you prefer to consume the data.

I find the breakdown handy for spotting outliers across all my ads. I can look at my CPC across all my ads in one big view, and see the age/gender groups that are breaking the bank. I can also see the ones that are cheap and interacting.

Some other things in here are the impressions, clicks, and cost per click by time zone. If you look at it for your time zone, what you may find is that there are certain times of day where you can get more eyeballs on your ads for less money.

For me, on the east coast, that usually starts at about 8 – 10 PM.

So, here's a little trick, nestled deep in this book for those of you who get this far: every night, at around 6 – 8 PM, I increase the spend on my best ads. Not by a lot. If I have an ad with a daily budget of $15, I might adjust it to $20; or if it's $35, I might bump it up to $42.

Then, come morning, I lower them back down. Yes, you guessed it: I do this every single day. Every. Single. Day.

You may be thinking, "Dear God! I don't have that kind of time; this guy spends at least an hour a day on his ads!"

Maybe not an hour, but some days, yes I do. My ads are the lifeblood of my sales. When Amazon's algorithms stop favoring a new book, I can keep it going with ads. Often, when Amazon's algorithms see a product page of mine that is converting well, they too will also promote that product, so ads can drive more sales straight from Amazon. They also keep you up in the ranks.

To that end, I try to squeeze every drop of performance from my ads that I can.

PART 6: NURTURING THAT GOOD AD

After you've done all the hard work getting that ad tuned and performing, you want it to keep performing, and performing better and better, right?

RIGHT?

I thought so. Sure, you can keep a little ad trickling along at $5/day and keep a series afloat. I've run some ads for folks with that spend, and they can keep a series with a $0.99 first book at about the 20,000 – 30,000 rank range with ease.

Now that's not too bad. If your series is five books long, and you have good read-through, that rank-range means you're probably making $30-$50 a day (if you're in KU). Even if only $10 a day of that is coming from ads, you're doubling your money every day.

Very few investments will yield returns like that.

But let's see if we can turn that knob up to 11, shall we?

MANAGING YOUR AD SPEND

You've diligently run your ad at $5/day to get that nice relevancy score, some shares and comments, and to settle into a good CPC. Now it's time to bump that spend up and get some magic happening!

Not so fast!

Here's the thing you need to consider: the audience you picked is only so big. At a higher spend rate, your ad may saturate the audience, and Facebook may start charging you a lot more per click because people start hiding your ad, or ignoring it.

You can see this as the frequency score on your ad. Close to 1 is good; if you're over 1.5, you're starting to saturate the audience.

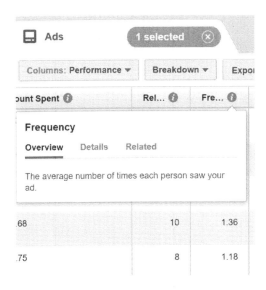

Because of this, it's best to up your ad spend by a few dollars every couple of days, as you fish out the sweet spot. I've found that with a lot of ads, you hit a point where you'll start to see that CPC begin to climb. It's often around $30-50 per day.

When you get to that point with an ad, it's time to start a new one and start warming it up, so that when your current heavyweight ad begins to lose effectiveness, you can boost it up.

I often have situations where one ad is on the way up, and another ad is on the way down, in terms of spend.

Also, if you read the end of Part 5, then you even know what time of day you should be doing that nice little incremental bump in spend.

SOCIAL PROOF

The Internet is awash with algorithms that try to determine whether or not humans will like a given thing. However, none of them are as good as *actual* humans for deciding what humans like.

To that end, Facebook still wants to know if actual people like a post. This is your "social proof".

Social proof on Facebook consists of likes, shares, and comments. The more likes, shares, and comments a post or ad has, the more social proof it has. Higher social proof means more relevancy, and FB will show it more, and charge you less for clicks.

In case you missed it before: Facebook does not do an all-out bidding war based on what you're willing to pay. There are people who will bid more for placement (or have more budget), but lose to you if you have a lower bid, but more social proof on your ad.

You can look at a long-running ad and see cost per click go down when you get comments and shares on your ad (likes to a lesser extent).

Part of why I bring this up is to temper excessive duplication of ads. While I encourage it so that you can hit specific groups of people with more targeted content, be sure that you don't spread your social proof too thin.

Keep this in mind as you build out more ads, especially on a limited budget where you're running multiple ads in an Ad Set.

A TRICK TO IMPROVE SOCIAL PROOF

As I've mentioned before, you can change the audience on an ad and not remove the likes, shares, or comments on that ad. This means an audience change doesn't lose your social proof.

Something I often do with ads is run them for the first few days targeted at my fans, and friends of my fans. Then, once I get good relevancy, some comments, likes, and shares, I alter my audience to *exclude* my fans.

COMMENTS

Previously, in one of the locations where I spoke about social proof, I mentioned that Facebook (by and large) considers all comments to be good comments. A healthy debate between two people (even if there is negativity and disagreement) is good business when your product is the discourse.

To that end, even "This books sucks poo poo" is a comment that boosts social proof for your ad.

That being said, you really don't want that on your ad, do you? What I do to comments like that is hide them, and let them live in their little echo chamber. Sometimes I hide them but respond (if the comment isn't too antagonistic).

However, just like you need a few 1-3 star reviews on your book, some lemon comments don't really hurt you much, either. In fact, they may help.

Right now I'm running a challenge ad where I say, "Is M. D. Cooper the next Larry Niven?" (for non-SF nerds, Larry Niven has been a Science Fiction titan since the early 70's).

That's a pretty tall order. I don't think I'm as good as Larry Niven, even on my best day. However, it has sparked some fun comments. Some I've hidden, but others I've engaged in, and we've discussed the merits of his books and mine.

Some comments had people saying that his stuff sucked and mine was great.

That being said, don't run challenge ads under your own Facebook author page. Those need to live under one of your fan/genre pages so that you can address the comments with your marketing/publicist hat on.

Also, just like 1-star reviews (yes, I respond to many of those), if that comment has burned your cookies, give it a day and see if it still bugs you enough to reply to it.

Whatever you do, don't get antagonistic with folks. Your readers are seeing your ads too, and they won't be happy if you come off like an ass.

PRODUCT PAGE TWEAKS

This is just a final little note that may help your product page convert just a bit better.

You're bound to have a particular ad that is your *main* ad at any given time. It may be character, plot, or even deal related. You want that ad to have a good flow into your product page so that the reader feels continuity.

To that end, what I recommend is for you to add a bit of text at the top of your blurb that connects your ad to the rest of your blurb.

For example, my book blurbs on my product pages are almost always character-based (talking about my main character and her challenges), but my best performing ad was plot-based, and the first paragraph of the blurb bore little resemblance to the ad.

To remedy this, I added in a bold paragraph that was a good grab line, and also connected to the ad.

This one change boosted my ad's conversion rate by 20%.

THE DEATH OF YOUR AD

All good ads go to heaven, so it's OK to kill that ad when its relevancy wanes, its CPC starts to climb, or its result rate diminishes.

I suspect you won't have too much trouble killing off dead ads, since they hit you in the wallet. However, those ads that ran long and did well can have a second life.

Take a look at the demographics you selected (be it male, female, country, age), and see if you can tweak the ad and give it new life by hitting a new demographic.

I recently had an ad that ran from November to May, and was finally getting to the end of its life. However, I looked at it and saw that I had made a silly mistake that caused it to have never shown in the UK

The mistake: I used a lookalike audience that was US-only as the foundation of the ad audience.

Well, well, well, I thought to myself, as I rubbed my hands together and quickly duplicated that ad with a UK-only target. Sure enough, there was this massive group of people across the pond that loved my ad.

That book has since moved from an average ranking of 12,000 to about 2500 in the UK store as a result. This book had been as high as 400 in the US store, but even then, its UK peak was 2400.

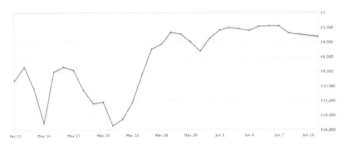

UK Sales Rank over the month. Down a bit now, which means I need to look at my audience saturation, but it's quite the jump!

That one little glance at a dying ad put a 5-year-old book into the top 2000 in the UK store.

Another option (which I also undertook) was to take the ad and retool its copy to be more character-based. Previously, that ad had bombed with women; but with this retooling, it did well (not amazing, but well), and has probably sold about 400 books at this point.

PART 7: BOOSTED POSTS

It would be remiss of me not to discuss boosted posts, as they are a great way to engage with your readers; but they are less effective at general advertising.

They're great for engaging with your readers, because you want them to know about new books coming out, new deals, promotions, upcoming books, etc... And all that works best when it comes right from you, in a very conversational voice.

Also, your readers know where to go to pick up your books, so your calls to action (CTAs) can be simple links at the bottom of the post.

One thing I must, once again, state as strongly as possible: Unless you're doing a cover reveal, the same image logic applies. Facebook will greatly prefer posts where the main image has no text.

I recently did a number of head-to-head tests on one of my fan pages, where I promoted a number of books for other authors. I did three with stock photos I picked up, and three with the book covers.

Facebook showed the ones with the stock photos 1500 times each. The ones that were just the book cover only got shown 300-400 times.

That's right: some of those posts reached 1/5 the people, just because I was lazy and didn't use a good picture. If ten of those missed 1200 people had bought the first book in a 5-book series, we know that the author missed out on at least $100 in read-through revenue. I later re-posted with better images.

So why don't they work as well for general ads? They're awesome when I focus on my fans and their friends!

The main reason is that there is no clear CTA (call to action), and that the image does not go to your destination.

Pretty simple, right?

On a purpose-built ad, the little link name in the lower left (usually AMAZON.COM), the CTA button on the lower right, *and* your image all go to your desired destination.

The Lost Colony Ship

In the spirit of great Space Opera by Peter F Hamilton, Jack Campbell, and Larry Niven comes Aeon 14. If you love strong heroines like Kris Longknife, then you're going to love Tanis Richards. Major Richards needs to get out of the Sol...

AMAZON.COM

Learn More

On a boosted post, clicking on the image just makes the image bigger. Your call to action is buried somewhere in your text, and looks like a link (and may look like a *messy* link), not a nice phrase.

Considering that there is nothing you can't do in an ad that a boosted post offers, I strongly suggest that you always do a regular ad when you're doing anything other than talking directly to your fans about some news or offer.

BONUS: TWITTER ADS

I've done some good work with Twitter ads, and while I find that they are not as effective (especially when it comes to long-running ads), they do have their uses.

I often run Twitter ads when I'm running a promo, or when a new book comes out; though I find them to be less effective when they run for long periods.

They also have a lower conversion rate, which is to say that they don't sell as many books per click; but I can also usually run them at only $0.05 - $0.10 per click, so that cost works out to some extent.

What I have found (anecdotally, since there is no way to properly measure this) is that Twitter ads seem to boost my page reads more than sales.

You can find Twitter ads in the upper right of the Twitter page, under your profile picture (just like Facebook!).

AUDIENCE

Twitter is pretty cool when it comes to selecting audiences. Essentially, if you can figure out someone's Twitter handle, you can target their followers. There are a number of traditional and indie authors who post on Twitter, and you can hunt them down and target their followers.

They also do have interests, but they're a much smaller list. I add them in, but my author targets seem to work better.

Like Facebook, they tell you the size of the audience you're targeting by using little dots.

One thing that works a lot better on Twitter is advertising to fans of TV shows and movies. However, this may be because of this little trick I use: all the big publishing houses have Twitter accounts. So, what I do there is I require that my targets also follow the big Sci-Fi/Fantasy publishers. I figure if people are following book publishers, they're serious book readers.

SPEND

This is critical. Twitter will nom nom nom all your money in hours, and give you squat for results. Unlike Facebook, where you want to let it do its auto-bid magic, on Twitter you *MUST* set a max bid.

I set my max bid at $0.20, sometimes even as low as $0.10. When I do this, Twitter suddenly behaves, and spends my money nice and evenly throughout the day.

Note: when you pick a max bid this low, Twitter will get all huffy and puffy and tell you with the red outline of doom that you have made a bad decision. Proceed to ignore them. It will be fine.

Set a daily maximum ❓ (required)

| $ | 20.00 | per day |

Set a total budget ❓ (optional)

| $ | None |

Choose pricing.

| Maximum bid ▾ | $ | 0.20 | per website click |

Other advertisers are bidding: $1.73 – $7.70

Low bid. Try bidding higher to ensure ad will show.

CREATIVE

On Facebook, your ad is called a 'Website Card'. These are formatted very close to how Facebook does them, with the exception of their 140 character limit and no text below the headline.

I should note that when you start making a Website Card, it says, "Create Tweet," which makes it seem like you're about to tweet right then and there. Don't worry; once you start typing, it pops up some other fields and looks like an ad creation form.

Twitter recommends (and I have found their recommendation to be sound) that you make multiple Website Cards per ad.

By the way, on Twitter, I have found that ads with book images work just as well as those without. So on Twitter, all that "no text, no book cover" advice goes out the window. Have at it.

REUSE

Twitter is kinda cool in that it lets you re-use the Website Cards on multiple ads. You can also edit them after the fact with no penalty.

They live inside this "Creatives" section up at the top.

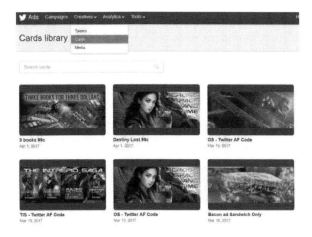

FINAL WORDS

There you have it: how to make some ads, and make some money on them—or at the very least, not lose too much money while you work out what works and what doesn't

Advertising is one of the oldest things around, but it's not solved. No one has all the answers, and it's constantly changing. Don't beat yourself up if you don't nail it the first time out.

But know your baseline thresholds, the max CPC you can tolerate, the base relevancy you should shoot for, and the number of clicks to get a sale.

Good baselines are

- Keep it under $0.30 cost per click (CPC)
- Relevancy of at least 8
- Shoot for at least one sale for every 30 clicks.

Remember, at $0.30 per click, and 30 clicks per sale, you're looking at $9 per sale; which means just one sale every 2 days (give or take a bit) when you're spending $5/day. However, in a series of books that have KU reads, that can be made back at around books 3 and 4 in the series.

That is also just a general threshold for what you want to shoot for. Your specific tolerances and measures for success will vary, but you *MUST* know what they are. And fail fast. Kill those bad ads in a day or two, not a week or two; tweak 'em, and make FB ads make you money.

THANK YOU

Thanks for taking the time to read this book. I really do hope it helps you out on your journey as an author.

As you all know, reviews are the best social proof a book can have, and I would greatly appreciate your review on this book.

Lastly, if you would like to stay informed about new things I learn, or any corrections and updates, sign up here:
http://eepurl.com/cPZdbv
(case sensitive)

Michael Cooper

36330604R00066

Printed in Great Britain
by Amazon